WHY DID THE PILGRIMS COME TO THE NEW WORLD?

And Other Questions about the Plymouth Colony

Laura Hamilton Waxman

LERNER PUBLICATIONS COMPANY · MINNEAPOLIS

A Word about Language
English word usage, spelling, grammar, and punctuation have changed over the centuries. We have preserved original spellings and word usage in the quotations included in this book.

Lerner Publications Company
A division of Lerner Publishing Group, Inc.
241 First Avenue North
Minneapolis, MN 55401 U.S.A.

Website address: www.lernerbooks.com

Library of Congress Cataloging-in-Publication Data

Waxman, Laura Hamilton.
    Why did the Pilgrims come to the New World? And other questions about the Plymouth Colony / by Laura Hamilton Waxman.
        p.   cm. — (Six questions of American history)
    Includes bibliographical references and index.
    ISBN 978–1–58013–665–5 (lib. bdg. : alk. paper)
    1. Mayflower Compact (1620)—Juvenile literature. 2. Pilgrims (New Plymouth Colony)—Juvenile literature. 3. Mayflower (Ship)—Juvenile literature.
    4. Massachusetts—History—New Plymouth, 1620–1691—Juvenile literature.
    I. Title.
F68.W38 2011
974.4'02—dc22   2009031518

Manufactured in the United States of America
1 – DP – 7/15/10

TABLE OF CONTENTS

THE SIX QUESTIONS HELP YOU DISCOVER THE FACTS!

INTRODUCTION

The *Mayflower* rocked gently on the Atlantic Ocean in the late fall of 1620. Cold November winds chilled the ship's crew working on the top deck. Below them, the *Mayflower*'s 102 passengers tried to stay warm in the leaky middle deck. These men, women, and children had been at sea for more than two months. They had left behind friends and family in England. They had suffered through violent storms and sickness. They had risked everything to start a new life in a new land.

Suddenly, someone on the top deck shouted and pointed into the distance. Land! Land had been spotted at last! News soon reached the passengers. They rejoiced and said a prayer of thanks. They had survived their ordeal at sea. But another, more dangerous adventure lay ahead of them.

The *Mayflower*'s passengers had come to North America to start an English colony. This new territory would be far from England but still under English rule. The colonists would have to start a new life in an unknown wilderness. To survive, they would have to work together and work hard.

These early colonists came to be known as the Pilgrims. Their story is one of courage and determination. But who were the Pilgrims?

A replica of the *Mayflower*

4

NORTH
AMERICA

PLYMOUTH
CAPE
COD

MAYFLOWER

IRELAND

ENGLAND
HOLLAND
LEIDEN

FRANCE

SPAIN

ATLANTIC
OCEAN

SOUTH
AMERICA

AFRICA

N

The Pilgrims
arrive at
Plymouth
Rock in this
painting from
the 1800s.

WHO
WHAT
WHERE
WHY
WHEN
HOW
WHO
WHAT
WHERE
WHY
WHEN
HOW
WHO
WHAT
WHERE
WHY
WHEN
HOW

This image from 1876 shows a Puritan family in England looking out across the Atlantic Ocean.

ONE SEEKING RELIGIOUS FREEDOM

The people we call the Pilgrims started out as lawbreakers in England. In about 1606, they formed a small Christian congregation, or religious group. They met secretly in the English farming town of Scrooby. There they worshipped according to their shared values and beliefs. Each time they gathered together, they risked jail or even death.

The Pilgrims knew that congregations such as theirs were illegal in England. The country had one official church. It was the Church of England, or Anglican Church. The nation's king or queen headed the Anglican Church. In 1606 King James I ruled England. He demanded that all

English citizens attend the Anglican Church. He expected the English people to believe what his church told them to believe.

But some citizens disagreed with the way the Anglican Church was run. These Anglicans became known as Puritans, from the word *purify.* They wanted to remain members of the church. But they also wanted to purify the church of practices and beliefs they disliked.

Other people separated from the church completely. They were called Separatists. Separatists formed their own illegal congregations. The Pilgrims' congregation in Scrooby was a Separatist congregation. Separatists such as the Pilgrims angered King James. He promised to punish them harshly for breaking the law. "I will make them conform," he announced, "or I will harry [harass] them out of the land!"

"I will make them conform, or I will harry [harrass] them out of the land!"

King James I of England

King James kept his word. In Scrooby, local officers spied on the Pilgrims' homes day and night. Some of their leaders were put in jail and forced to pay fines. Still, the congregation refused to give in to the king's demands.

The Pilgrims knew that other Separatists had fled to Holland. This Dutch country offered the only religious freedom in Europe. In Holland, people could worship as they pleased. The Pilgrims discussed moving to Holland too. But moving meant leaving behind their family, friends, and homes. It meant learning a new language and getting used to a new way of life.

Yet life for the Pilgrims had become unbearable under King James's

WHAT DOES PILGRIM MEAN?

The word *pilgrim* refers to a person who travels to a sacred place for a religious purpose. The first person to describe the Puritans as pilgrims was William Bradford. He was an English Separatist from Scrooby. He called his people pilgrims because they had traveled a great distance for their religion. Even so, he never meant for the community to be called the Pilgrims. But the name caught on.

rule. In 1607 more than half the congregation's members decided to flee their homeland. They sold their houses and packed their belongings. King James had blocked all Separatists from legally leaving the country. So the Pilgrims also hired a ship to sneak them across the English Channel.

The Pilgrims met their ship in the dead of night. They paid the captain and got on board. But they never set sail. The captain had secretly warned local officials of their plan to escape. The officials showed up at the last minute and dragged the Pilgrims off to jail.

The Pilgrims refused to be discouraged. By the summer of 1608, most of them had managed to get out of England. They reunited in the Dutch city of Amsterdam. In 1609 they moved to another Dutch city called Leiden. The Pilgrims rejoiced in their newfound freedom. At last they could worship together without fear.

When they weren't praying, the Pilgrims were working. They spent many backbreaking hours spinning wool, weaving cloth, or making hats. Even so, most of them barely earned enough money to survive.

WHERE IS LEIDEN, HOLLAND?
It is about 20 miles (30 kilometers) southwest of Amsterdam.

Haarlem
Amsterdam
Leiden
Utrecht
Rotterdam

GPS

After nine years, the Pilgrims began questioning their decision to live in Holland. They still valued their religious freedom. But they didn't like being so poor. Even worse, some of their children had begun taking on Dutch ways. The Pilgrims worried that their families might lose their English and Separatist values. They had also heard rumors of an oncoming war between Holland and Spain. Spain was a Catholic country. The Pilgrims feared that Spain would take control of Holland. Then Spain's Catholic king might end the Pilgrims' religious freedom.

Catholic: a form of Christianity that follows the teachings of the Roman Catholic Church

King Philip III of Spain

This church in the Dutch city of Rotterdam is known as the Pilgrim Fathers' Church. The church was named in honor of the Separtists.

But where else could they go? Returning to England was out of the question. Other countries in Europe wouldn't welcome them either. Then someone in the congregation suggested a bold idea. Perhaps they should settle a new English colony in the New World.

the term early colonists used to describe the Americas and other newly settled lands

NEXT QUESTION

WHY DID THE PILGRIMS WANT TO START A COLONY IN THE NEW WORLD?

Colonists begin building the first English settlement at Jamestown in 1607.

TWO OFF TO THE NEW WORLD

The Pilgrims called the Americas the New World for a reason. To them and other Europeans, it was a strange and unknown land. At the time, only one English colony existed in all of North America. Jamestown had been colonized in 1607. It was located in an area of English land known as the Virginia Territory. The Virginia Territory included the modern-day states of Virginia, Ohio, Kentucky, Illinois, Indiana, and Wisconsin.

The Pilgrims in Holland had heard of Jamestown's struggles. In its first years, dozens of colonists had died of disease and starvation. The newcomers were also attacked

WHERE IS THE VIRGINIA TERRITORY?

The U.S. states shown in red were once part of England's Virginia Territory.

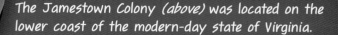

The Jamestown Colony (above) was located on the lower coast of the modern-day state of Virginia.

by Native Americans who wanted them off their land. Millions of Native Americans had lived in the Americas for thousands of years. But Europeans knew little about them.

Some Pilgrims thought it was crazy to risk their lives in the New World. Others believed going there was their best choice. These Pilgrims argued for a new English town in North America. There they could create the exact sort of community they longed for. The community's members would share the same beliefs and values. They wouldn't have to worry about foreign customs or an angry King James. After much debate, some members of the congregation decided to take the risk.

For two years, the Pilgrims prepared for their travels to North America. They had to hire two ships and captains to take them there. And the Pilgrims had to fill those ships with many supplies. The Pilgrims needed enough food and drink to last the 3,000-mile (4,800 km) journey. They needed tools for farming and building homes. They needed seeds for planting and farm animals such as chickens, sheep, and goats. And they needed weapons to protect them against possible Native American enemies. They even hired a military leader named Miles (sometimes spelled Myles) Standish. His job was to help them defend their new colony.

All this cost much more money than the Pilgrims had. They sought help from a group of men in London known as the Merchant Adventurers. These

Miles Standish

merchants, or business owners, agreed to help pay for the Pilgrims' journey and settlement. In return, the Pilgrims agreed to pay back the Merchant Adventurers with furs, fish, wood, and other valuable goods from North America.

The Merchant Adventurers did something equally important. They helped the Pilgrims get a document called a land patent. The patent gave the Pilgrims the right to claim a section of land in England's Virginia Territory. It also meant that the colony would be under the protection of the English government.

a document that gives a person or group control or ownership of something

Pilgrims board their ships in 1620 in this painting by Adam van Breen (1590–1645).

In July 1620, fifty-seven Pilgrims stepped onto a small ship called the *Speedwell*. Many of them cried as they waved good-bye to their friends standing onshore. They knew they might never see one another again.

The *Speedwell* set off from Holland for England. There it met with a larger ship, the *Mayflower*. A second group of new passengers were also waiting to sail on the *Mayflower*. Some of these newcomers were friends and family of the Pilgrims. Many of them held similar religious beliefs. But other passengers had been sent by the Merchant Adventurers to help make the colony a success. The Pilgrims called these passengers Strangers. The Strangers had not chosen to go to the New World for religious freedom. They simply wanted a chance at a new life. In return, they agreed to remain loyal to the new colony and to work for its success.

The *Mayflower* and the *Speedwell* set sail from England on August 5, 1620. But the *Speedwell* turned out to be a leaky ship. Both ships had to turn back twice so that

WHAT U.S. DOCUMENT PROTECTS RELIGIOUS FREEDOM?

In modern times, millions of people have come to the United States from all over the world. Many of these immigrants have sought religious freedom, just as the Pilgrims did. The Bill of Rights protects this freedom. The Bill of Rights is part of the U.S. Constitution. It includes ten important rights. Freedom of religion is the first right listed.

Passengers aboard the *Mayflower* wave farewell as they set off for the New World. This print is based on a painting by Gustave Alaux.

the *Speedwell* could be repaired. Finally, the Pilgrims decided to leave the smaller ship behind. Some of the Pilgrims decided to stay behind too. The rest of the 102 passengers stuffed themselves into the *Mayflower*'s middle deck.

The *Mayflower* left Plymouth, England, once again on September 6, 1620. Captain Christopher Jones steered the ship out onto the open ocean. Autumn was a bad season to be traveling by sea. Violent ocean winds and storms were common at that time of year. The *Mayflower* would be in for a rough ride.

NEXT QUESTION

WHEN DID THE PILGRIMS FIRST CATCH SIGHT OF THE NEW WORLD?

This painting by American artist Gilbert Tucker Margeson (1852–1949) depicts the *Mayflower* at sea. Storms at sea, cramped quarters, and lack of fresh food and water made the long journey seem even longer.

THREE STRUGGLES AT SEA

Day after day, passengers stayed in the damp, dark middle deck. They fed on hard biscuits, salted meat, and weak beer. They had no fresh food or fresh water. To make matters worse, the ship was often thrown about on the choppy seas. Many of the passengers suffered from terrible seasickness. It didn't help that the middle deck stunk of dirty bodies and farm animals.

The passenger deck was less than 5 feet (1.5 meters) high and only 75 feet (23 m) long. In such cramped quarters, the passengers got on one another's nerves. They had little privacy and often argued with one another.

seasickness dizziness and upset stomach caused by the rocking motion of a ship in water

The Inside of the *Mayflower*

Labels on diagram:
- masts
- chart house
- main deck
- middle deck
- hull
- waterline
- main hold

The differences between the Pilgrims and some of the Strangers grew. Everyone longed for space, fresh air, and land beneath their feet. After sixty-five days, their wish was granted. The *Mayflower* came within sight of land on November 9, 1620.

The *Mayflower II* is a copy of the ship that brought the Pilgrims to North America. The *Mayflower II* was built in the 1950s. It is part of the historical museum at Plimouth Plantation in Massachusetts.

The passengers scrambled to the top deck to catch a glimpse of their new home. William Bradford wrote, "The appearance of it [North America] much comforted us. . . . It caused us to rejoice together and praise God."

This ship was heading toward modern-day Massachusetts. Captain Jones promised to take his passengers south to the Virginia Territory. That way, the Pilgrims could honor their land patent and have a legal English colony.

The captain guided the ship down along the coast. But he soon ran into trouble. The *Mayflower* came to a deadly section of shoreline called Pollack Rip. Violent waves smashed into the ship and nearly sank it. The *Mayflower* would never be able to pass through. Captain Jones turned back the ship just in time. He anchored it off the coast of Cape Cod in Massachusetts. The Pilgrims would have to set up their colony north of the Virginia Territory after all.

This change of plans caused an uproar among the passengers. Some of the Strangers argued for a split from the Pilgrims. After all, they said, the Pilgrims' land patent no longer held any power.

a peninsula, or piece of land, connected to the modern-day state of Massachusetts and surrounded by the Atlantic Ocean

WHERE IS THE POLLOCK RIP?
This stretch of water is south of Cape Cod. At the Rip, water flowing in and out of Nantucket Sound meets the open ocean.

Provincetown

Plymouth

Cape Cod Bay

Barnstable Town

Pollock Rip Channel

GPS

That meant the Strangers' promise of loyalty held no power either. These Strangers said they had the right to strike out on their own.

Right away, some of the passengers saw the danger of this. They argued for the need to stick together. Survival was not possible unless everyone worked together, they said. Did they all want to die as so many of the colonists in Jamestown had?

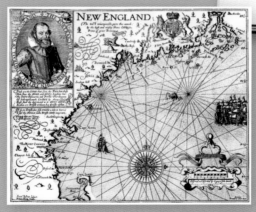

After much debate, the passengers agreed to stay united. They wrote an agreement that became known as the Mayflower Compact. The compact laid out a simple plan of government. It said that the *Mayflower* passengers promised to be loyal to the new colony. That meant respecting the colony's leaders and obeying its laws.

an agreement between two or more groups of people. The Mayflower Compact was an agreement between the Pilgrims and the Strangers.

WHAT WAS THE PURPOSE OF THE MAYFLOWER COMPACT?

The Mayflower Compact created the first government of its kind in America. Like our modern government, this colonial government got its power from its people. That meant the people of Plymouth Colony chose their leaders and their laws. The original Mayflower Compact no longer exists. But William Bradford kept a record of this important agreement. Here is part of what it says:

We, whose names are underwritten...do by these Presents, solemnly and mutually, in the Presence of God and one another, covenant and combine ourselves together into a civil Body Politick, for our better Ordering and Preservation, and Furtherance of the Ends aforesaid: And by Virtue hereof do enact, constitute, and frame, such just and equal Laws, Ordinances, Acts, Constitutions, and Officers, from time to time, as shall be thought most meet and convenient for the general Good of the Colony; unto which we promise all due Submission and Obedience.

The Mayflower Compact

In return, the colony's leaders had to treat the people fairly. And the colony's laws had to be reasonable and just.

The *Mayflower's* adult male passengers signed the compact on November 11. Then they elected their colony's governor. They chose a Pilgrim named John Carver.

The passengers had another important task ahead of them. They needed to choose a good place to settle. And they needed to do it soon. December was approaching. They had nearly run out of food and drink. If they didn't start building their colony soon, they might not survive the winter.

NEXT QUESTION

HOW DID THE PILGRIMS FEEL ABOUT THE NATIVE AMERICANS WHO LIVED IN NEW ENGLAND?

Men from the *Mayflower* rowed ashore at Cape Cod to explore the new land.

FOUR: SEARCH FOR A NEW HOME

A small group of men from the *Mayflower* rowed a boat toward the shore of Cape Cod. In front of them lay a strange and wild land. Behind them stretched 3,000 miles (4,828 km) of cold sea. Bitter November winds whipped about them. Seawater splashed into the boat and froze on their clothes. By the time they reached land, many of the men were shaking and sneezing.

They were relieved to finally set foot on solid ground. At the same time, they felt utterly alone. As William Bradford wrote, "They had now no friends to wellcome them, nor inns to entertain or refresh their weatherbeaten bodys,

> **"They had now no friends to wellcome them, nor inns to entertaine or refresh their weatherbeaten bodys, no houses or much less townes to repaire [go] too, to seeke for succoure [help and comfort]."**

William Bradford

no houses or much less townes to repaire [go] too, to seeke for succoure [help and comfort]."

For about a month, the male passengers took turns searching Cape Cod for a place to settle. They always carried weapons wherever they went. The Pilgrims were uneasy about the people who already lived in the area. Would these Native Americans be friendly? Or would they dislike the white strangers?

WHAT DID THE PILGRIMS THINK OF THEIR NEIGHBORS?

The Pilgrims' ideas about Native Americans came from the writings of European explorers. The explorers often described the native people as frightening and strange. Europeans did not understand the way Native Americans spoke, acted, or dressed. They did not understand Native American customs and traditions. And they didn't realize that millions of Native Americans had been living in the Americas long before any Europeans arrived. Instead, these explorers presented the New World as an empty land. They said it was ready to be claimed by new colonists. All of these ideas affected the way the Pilgrims reacted to the Native Americans they met.

(NAW–sehts)
a Native American group that lived in Massachusetts and part of Cape Cod

The local Native Americans were the Nausets. The Pilgrims caught glimpses of Nauset people from time to time. But these locals always ran from them.

The Pilgrims also came across some of the Nausets' empty wigwams. These dome-shaped houses were probably the Nausets' summer homes. Most likely, the Native American community had already moved inland to their winter homes.

The Pilgrims did not always treat these summer homes with respect. One day they came across an empty wigwam and farm. They discovered baskets of dried corn buried underground. A Nauset family had stored this corn for the winter. Come planting time, it would be seed for new plants. The Pilgrims feared they might starve without corn seed of their own. They took away as much of the buried corn as they could carry.

Another day they entered a different wigwam. They

This modern photo shows a traditional wigwam. Round wigwams covered in tree bark were used by Nausets and other northeastern Native Americans.

This hand-colored woodcut shows the Pilgrims and Native Americans fighting with guns and bows and arrows on Cape Cod in December 1620.

searched inside and took everything that might help them survive. They left no payment or peace offering behind.

The Nausets had been watching the Pilgrims from hidden lookouts. The actions of the white strangers angered them. Without warning, they attacked a group of settlers on the morning of December 7. The Pilgrims fought back. In the end, the Nauset fighters fled before anyone got hurt. This event became known as the First Encounter (meeting).

The Pilgrims decided to leave Cape Cod soon after the First Encounter. The land was too sandy for good farming. And they had made enemies of the local people. They decided to go up the coast to Plymouth Harbor. They hoped to find a good place to settle there.

a protected body of water on the coast of Massachusetts

NEXT QUESTION

HOW DID THE PILGRIMS FINALLY SET UP THEIR NEW COLONY?

Pilgrims searched for a good place to settle after arriving in Plymouth in December 1620.

FIVE SETTLING PLYMOUTH COLONY

A few men set off in a boat for Plymouth Harbor. The rest of the passengers stayed on the *Mayflower* near Cape Cod. These men, women, and children shared what little food was left. They struggled to stay warm through snowstorms. Some of the passengers started to fall ill. A few even died.

The small boat landed at Plymouth Harbor on December 11, 1620. Once again, the Pilgrims set about exploring the land. To their relief, they found a promising site for a colony. It lay on high ground not too far from shore. The site was close enough to the sea for fishing and travel.

And it was high enough to protect the colony from flooding. Further inland rose an even higher hill. From there, a person could see many miles into the distance. This would serve as an excellent lookout.

Just as important were the brooks that ran through the land. They would supply the colonists with much-needed drinking water. The Pilgrims also discovered that much of the land had already been cleared for farming. Yet the Pilgrims saw no homes or sign of human life. Plymouth appeared to be theirs for the taking. The men sent for the rest of the passengers on the *Mayflower*. The time had finally come to start their new colony.

The Pilgrims come ashore from the *Mayflower* after choosing Plymouth as a suitable place to settle.

With winter coming, the Pilgrims worked hard to build shelter in Plymouth. They used local trees for timber.

Everyone took part in the hard work of settling into their new village. They named it New Plymouth. It became known as the Plymouth Colony. By December 25, they had begun to build their common house. This building was to be used for meetings and storage. The colonists planned to build eighteen more houses for individual families. But they didn't get very far.

In January a deadly illness took hold of the colony. The sickness probably came about from cold weather, poor food, and exhaustion. Nearly all the colonists fell ill. Only six or seven of them remained healthy. These healthy ones cared for the sick as best they could. Even so, they couldn't stop many of the colonists from dying. Sometimes two or three people died in one day. By spring nearly half of them were dead.

The survivors began to recover in the warmer weather of spring. They began once again to build homes for a town. As they worked, they sometimes saw or heard Native Americans in the distance. But the Native Americans never came close.

Then on March 16, a tall Native American man walked right up to some of the settlers. To their surprise, he spoke to them in English.

This print from the late 1800s shows the Pilgrims going to church services at the common house. They suffered through bitter cold and deadly sicknesses during their first winter in Plymouth.

"Welcome, Englishmen!" he said.

His name was Samoset. He was an Abenaki from modern-day Maine. Samoset said he had learned English from fur trappers and fishers who came from England each year. These men often traded with the Native Americans they encountered.

The Pilgrims were glad to meet a Native American who could talk with them. They asked Samoset about the Native Americans who lived in the area. Samoset told the Pilgrims that the Wampanoag lived nearby. Their leader was named Massasoit.

This illustration shows Samoset visiting the Pilgrims in the Plymouth Colony.

WHAT IS PLYMOUTH ROCK?

Legend says that the Pilgrims first landed on a spot known as Plymouth Rock. Famous paintings show men and women scrambling onto this large boulder in Plymouth Harbor. But no Pilgrim ever wrote about such a landing. In fact, they never mentioned Plymouth Rock at all. The story of Plymouth Rock first came to light more than one hundred years after the Pilgrims came to Plymouth. Most historians believe the legend is probably untrue. However, a boulder called Plymouth Rock does exist. A part of it sits on the shore of the modern town of Plymouth, Massachusetts. And it is a popular tourist attraction.

The Pilgrims had learned their lesson with the Nausets. This time, they wanted to start things off on the right foot. They told Samoset they wished to make peace with the Wampanoag. Samoset agreed to help them. In the meantime, the Pilgrims could only hope for the best.

NEXT QUESTION

WHAT EVENT IN THE PILGRIMS' HISTORY INSPIRED OUR THANKSGIVING HOLIDAY?

Native Americans offer a deer to the Plymouth colonists in this print.

SIX GIVING THANKS

The Wampanoags had once been a large and powerful Native American community. But in 1617, a terrible sickness killed thousands of them. The illness came from germs spread by Europeans in North America. Entire Native American villages were wiped out. One of those villages stood on what had become Plymouth Colony. The Wampanoags had called it Patuxet.

On March 22, 1621, Samoset returned with four men from Massasoit's village. One of them was named Squanto. Squanto spoke even better English than Samoset. The Pilgrims soon learned that he was the only survivor from Patuxet.

WHO WAS SQUANTO?

Squanto's life story is a sad one. In 1614 an Englishman kidnapped him and several other Native Americans. The man took them to Spain and sold them as slaves. Squanto managed to gain his freedom. He ended up in London, England, where he learned to speak English. Eventually, he found a ship that took him back to North America. When he returned home, he discovered that his family and friends in Patuxet were all dead. He lived in Massasoit's village before the Pilgrims arrived. After that, he lived in Plymouth until his death in 1622.

Squanto told the Pilgrims that Massasoit wanted to meet with them. Squanto also agreed to act as an interpreter. He would help Massasoit and the Pilgrims talk with one another.

Massasoit and some of his warriors came to Plymouth that same day. The Pilgrims offered the Wampanoag leader gifts of friendship. They also gave him some of what little food they had.

interpreter: a person who translates for groups of people who speak different languages. An interpreter can speak two or more languages and can tell each group what the other is saying.

Massasoit and other Wampanoag leaders visited the Plymouth Colony in March 1621.

Massasoit agreed to speak with Plymouth's leader, John Carver. Squanto helped the two men work out a peace treaty, or agreement. The treaty said that the Wampanoag and the colonists promised to maintain a friendly relationship. It also said that they would defend each other against any enemies.

The two leaders signed the agreement by the end of that day. Then Massasoit and his men went back to their village. Only Squanto stayed behind. He agreed to live with the Pilgrims in what had once been his village.

This illustration shows Massasoit and Pilgrim leaders agreeing to a treaty.

Squanto turned out to be very valuable to the Pilgrims. He taught them how to catch eel (a type of fish) and seafood. He showed them where to find wild fruits and other useful plants. And he showed them how to plant corn. Squanto told the settlers to mix dead fish into the earth. The fish added important nutrients to the soil. Otherwise, he said, the corn plants would not grow well.

On April 5, the *Mayflower* set sail for its return to England. The colonists were truly on their own. There was no way to go back home or send for more supplies. And the nearest English colony, Jamestown, was hundreds of miles away.

About a week later, Governor Carver fell ill suddenly and died. Without a leader, the colony could have fallen apart. But the Mayflower Compact kept that from happening. The signers of the compact stayed true to their agreement.

Together they chose a new governor for their colony. He was thirty-two-year-old William Bradford.

The colonists spent their days hunting and fishing, tending crops, and building houses. Slowly, they created new lives for themselves in their new home. By fall it was time to harvest their crops. The Pilgrims had planted peas and barley from England. Those crops hadn't grown well in the soil of New England. But their corn had grown tall thanks to Squanto.

Back in England, the colonists would have celebrated the harvest with a feast and a festival. The Pilgrims decided to do something similar

> "I never in my life remember a more seasonable year than we have here enjoyed."
>
> —Edward Winslow, writing to a friend in England after the Pilgrims' first harvest

in their new home. They invited their new Wampanoag neighbors to join them.

Ninety Wampanoags took part in the celebration at Plymouth. For three days, the colonists and Indians feasted together. They also played games and practiced shooting at targets with guns and arrows. This celebration probably took place in September or October. Later, it came to be thought of as the first Thanksgiving. It marked the first year of the colony's survival.

Plymouth Colony went on to last another seventy years. During that time, other ships

Thanksgiving: a traditional holiday that celebrates good fortune. In the modern United States, Thanksgiving is celebrated on the fourth Thursday in November.

The Plymouth Colony celebrated its first harvest in the fall of 1621. The Pilgrims and Wampanoags shared food and played games. J. L. G. Ferris painted his view of this event in the early 1900s.

WHAT WAS EATEN AT THE FIRST THANKSGIVING?

A Pilgrim named Edward Winslow wrote about Plymouth's first harvest festival in 1621. He described a celebration very different from our modern Thanksgiving. The Pilgrims and Native Americans ate goose, duck, and deer. They probably ate outside around open fires.

arrived with more colonists from England. Some of the newcomers were Separatists. Many others were not. Together, they expanded the colony from one struggling village to twenty-one farming towns.

Throughout the 1600s, thousands of other English people came to New England as well. Many of them were Puritans seeking religious freedom as the Pilgrims had.

One of the Puritans' most successful settlements was called Massachusetts Bay Colony. It included the town of Boston.

William Bradford remained governor of Plymouth for most of his life. He tried to lead the colony with a fair but firm hand. He also kept peaceful relations with Massasoit and the Wampanoag. But the Plymouth Colony fought battles with other Native American communities.

The worst fighting took place after Bradford and Massasoit had both died. Massasoit's son Metacom became the Wampanoags' new leader in 1662. The English colonists knew him as King Philip. King Philip was angered by how much land the English colonists had taken in Massachusetts. He turned the Wampanoags and other Native American communities against colonies such as Plymouth.

In 1675 war broke out between the colonists and the local Native Americans. The war became known as King Philip's War. It lasted until the following year. Hundreds of colonists and thousands of Native Americans died in the fighting.

Metacom, or King Philip

A museum and history center marks the site of the Plymouth Colony in modern-day Massachusetts. In this photo, tourists walk between rows of houses built to look like the Pilgrims' homes.

Plymouth Colony survived another fourteen years after the war. In 1691 it became part of the Massachusetts Bay Colony. Eventually, Plymouth became a town in the state of Massachusetts.

The Pilgrims' colony ended long before the United States became a nation. Yet their story was not forgotten. It has remained an important part of U.S. history.

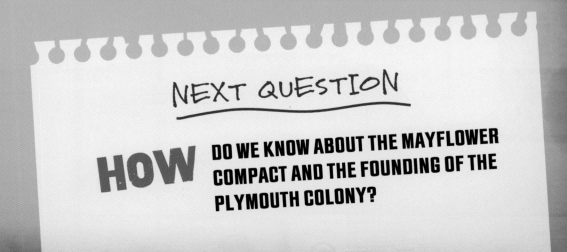

NEXT QUESTION

HOW DO WE KNOW ABOUT THE MAYFLOWER COMPACT AND THE FOUNDING OF THE PLYMOUTH COLONY?

Primary Source: William Bradford's Journal

Much of what we know about the Pilgrims comes from William Bradford. In 1622 he published his journal of the Pilgrims' experience in the New World. He also finished a longer history of the colony in 1650. Other Pilgrims, such as Edward Winslow, left behind writings about their experiences too. The colony also kept detailed records of its citizens. All these papers are important primary sources.

A primary source is a document written by a person who was alive at the time of an event. It is often a firsthand description of something that happened in history. Letters, journals, and newspaper articles are examples of primary sources. The following primary source is a section from Bradford's journal. It describes the first time a small group of Pilgrims set foot on Plymouth.

> After our landing and viewing of the places, so well as we....set on the maine Land, on the first place, on an high ground, where there is a great deale of Land cleared, and hath beene planted with Corne three or four yeares agoe, and there is a very sweet brooke runnes vnder the hill side, and many delicate springs of as good water as can be drunke, and where we may harbour our Shallops and Boates exceeding well, and in this brooke much good fish in their seasons: on the further side of the river also much Corne ground cleared; in one field is a great hill....from thence we may see into the Bay, and farre into the Sea, and we may see thence Cape Cod: our greatest labour will be fetching of our wood, which is halfe a quarter of an English myle, but there is enough so farre off; what people inhabite here we yet know not, for as yet we haue scene none.

TELL YOUR PILGRIM STORY

You are a Pilgrim who has recently arrived in the New World. You are busy settling the Plymouth Colony and making a new life for yourself. Write a journal entry or letter home describing your experiences.

WHO are you? (Are you a boy, girl, man, or woman? Are you a Pilgrim or a Stranger?)

WHERE are you originally from?

WHY have you come to Plymouth?

WHEN did you arrive?

WHAT is your new home like?

WHAT is the weather like?

HOW do you spend your days?

HOW do you get along with the other colonists?

USE **WHO, WHAT, WHERE WHY, WHEN,** AND **HOW** TO THINK OF OTHER QUESTIONS TO HELP YOU CREATE YOUR STORY!

Timeline

ca. 1606

A group of Christians (later called Pilgrims) break with the Church of England and form a secret congregation in Scrooby, England.

1607

Jamestown, the first English colony in North America, is settled.

The Pilgrims try to flee England for Holland. They are caught and jailed.

1608

The Pilgrims make more attempts to get to Holland. They finally reach the Dutch city of Amsterdam.

1609

The Pilgrims set up a congregation in the **Dutch city of Leiden.**

1617

The Pilgrims begin making plans to go to the New World.

1619

The Merchant Adventurers help the Pilgrims get a patent to set up a colony in the Virginia Territory.

1620

In July, the Pilgrims leave Holland on the *Speedwell*. They meet up with the *Mayflower* in England.

On August 5, the *Speedwell* and the *Mayflower* set off from England for the New World. The *Speedwell* leaks, and both ships turn back.

The *Mayflower* sets off on September 6 for the New World.

On November 9, *Mayflower* passengers see the eastern coast of North America for the first time.

The *Mayflower*'s adult male passengers sign the Mayflower Compact. They elect John Carver as their first governor on November 11. Some of the settlers begin exploring Cape Cod.

On December 7, the Nausets of Cape Cod attack a group of Pilgrims who have stolen from them. The event is called the First Encounter.

After this First Encounter, the Pilgrims leave Cape Cod. They choose Plymouth as the place to start their new colony.

1621

Nearly half of the colonists die of illness in the first three months of the year. The surviving colonists meet Squanto. He comes from a nearby Wampanoag village.

In March, Wampanoag leader Massasoit and Governor John Carver sign a peace treaty.

On April 5, the *Mayflower* returns to England.

Later that month, Carver dies. The colonists choose **William Bradford** to be their new governor.

In the fall, the colonists invite their Wampanoag neighbors to a harvest feast. It is later called the First Thanksgiving.

In November thirty-five new colonists arrive in Plymouth aboard the *Fortune*. It is the first of several ships that bring new colonists over the years.

1622

Squanto dies.

1630s

Plymouth colony begins to expand. In time, it grows to twenty-one farming towns. Other English colonies begin to form in New England.

1657

William Bradford dies after serving as governor for most of his life.

1660

Massasoit dies. His and Bradford's deaths lead to an end of peaceful relations between the Plymouth colonists and the Wampanoag.

1675–1676

Plymouth Colony takes part in King Philip's War.

1691

Plymouth Colony becomes part of Massachusetts Bay Colony.

Source Notes

7 George F. Willison, *Saints and Strangers* (New York: Reynal & Hitchcock, 1945), 48.

7 Ibid.

19 William Bradford, in *Mourt's Relation: A Journal of the Pilgrims at Plymouth* (1622; repr. New York: Corinth Books, 1963), 15.

22 William Bradford, *History of Plymouth Plantation* (Boston: Little Brown Co., 1856), 90.

24–25 Ibid., 78.

25 Ibid.

38 Edward Winslow, in *Mourt's Relation: A Journal of the Pilgrims at Plymouth* (1622; The Plymouth Colony Archive Project, 2000–2007), http://www.histarch.uiuc.edu/plymouth/mourt6.html.

42 George B. Cheever, *The Journal of the Pilgrims at Plymouth, in New England, in 1620: Reprinted from the Original Volume with Historical and Local Illustrations of Providences, Principles and Persons.* (New York: Wiley, 1848), 49.

Selected Bibliography

Bradford, William. *History of Plymouth Plantation.* Boston, Little Brown & Co., 1856. Available online at http://books.google.com/books?id=tYecOAN1cwwC&printsec=frontcover&dq=william+bradford (July 22, 2009).

Deetz, Jim, and Patricia Scott Deetz. *The Times of Their Lives: Life, Love, and Death in Plymouth Colony.* New York: W. H. Freeman, 2000.

Hodgson, Godfrey. *A Great and Godly Adventure: The Pilgrims and the Myth of the First Thanksgiving.* New York: PublicAffairs, 2006.

Langdon, George D., Jr. *Pilgrim Colony: A History of New Plymouth 1620–1691.* New Haven, CT: Yale University Press, 1966.

Mourt's Relation: A Journal of the Pilgrims at Plymouth. 1622. Reprint, New York: Corinth Books, 1963.

Philbrick, Nathaniel. *Mayflower: A Story of Courage, Community and War.* New York: Viking, 2006.

Stratton, Eugene Aubrey. *Plymouth Colony, Its History and People, 1620–1691.* Salt Lake City: Ancestry Pub., 1986.

Willison, George F. *Saints and Strangers.* New York: Reynal & Hitchcock, 1945.

Further Reading and Websites

Arenstam, Peter, John Kemp, and Catherine O'Neill Grace. *Mayflower 1620: A New Look at a Pilgrim Voyage*. Washington, DC: National Geographic Children's Books, 2007. This book uses photographs and text to re-create this famous journey to the New World.

Bial, Raymond. *The Wampanoag*. New York: Benchmark Books, 2004. The author describes the customs, history, and lives of the Wampanoag Indian nation.

Harness, Cheryl. *The Adventurous Life of Myles Standish and the Amazing-but-True Survival Story of the Plymouth Colony*. Washington, DC: National Geographic, 2006. This biography of Miles Standish focuses on his leadership of the Plymouth Colony.

Kessel, Joyce K. *Squanto and the First Thanksgiving*. Minneapolis: Millbrook Press, 2004. This illustrated story shows how Squanto helped the Pilgrims survive their first year in Plymouth.

Miller, Brandon Marie. *Growing Up in a New World*. Minneapolis: Lerner Publications, 2003. How would it feel to cross an ocean in search of a new life? Miller looks at the lives of children and young people in early colonial America.

Pilgrim Hall Museum
http://www.pilgrimhall.org/plgrmhll.htm
This museum's site is full of information about the Pilgrims and Thanksgiving.

Plimoth for Kids
http://www.plimoth.org/kids/
This section of the Plimoth Plantation Museum's website includes recipes, stories, and helpful information about life in the Plymouth Colony.

The 13 Colonies
http://www.socialstudiesforkids.com/graphics/13mapnew.htm
A clickable map leads visitors to information about each of the original thirteen British colonies in North America, including Massachusetts.

Waters, Kate. *Samuel Eaton's Day: A Day in the Life of a Pilgrim Boy*. New York: Scholastic Paperbacks, 1996, and *Sarah Morton's Day: A Day in the Life of a Pilgrim Girl*. New York: Scholastic Paperbacks, 1993. Each book is told from the point of view of a child living in the Plymouth Colony.

Index

Photo Acknowledgments

The images in this book are used with the permission of: © iStockphoto.com/DNY59, p. 1;
© iStockphoto.com/Skip O'Donnell, pp. 1 (background) and all wooden floor backgrounds;
© iStockphoto.com/sx70, pp. 3 (top), 8 (bottom), 16, 21 (right), 25 (bottom), 33 (top), 35 (top), 39
(bottom); © iStockphoto.com/Ayse Nazli Deliormanli, pp. 3 (bottom), 43 (left); © iStockphoto.com/Serdar
Yagci, pp. 4-5 (background), 22 (background), 43 (background); © iStockphoto.com/Andrey Pustovoy,
pp. 4, 11 (top), 19 (bottom), 26, 41 (top); © Joe Sohm/VisionsofAmerica/Photodisc/Getty Images, p. 4
(inset); © Bill Hauser/Independent Picture Service, pp. 4-5, 9 (inset), 13 (inset), 19 (top), 20 (inset);
© Bridgeman-Giraudon/Art Resource, NY, p. 5 (bottom left); © Bettmann/CORBIS, p. 6; © Paul van
Somer/The Bridgeman Art Library/Getty Images, p. 7; © Time & Life Pictures/Getty Images, p. 8 (top);
© iStockphoto.com/Talshiar, pp. 9, 13 (left), 20; The Art Archive/Museo del Prado Madrid/Alfredo Dagli
Orti, p. 10; © Jon Hicks/CORBIS, p. 11 (inset); © North Wind Picture Archives, pp. 12, 14 (bottom),
21 (left), 24, 27 (top), 29, 30, 32, 34, 35 (bottom), 36, 40; © MPI/Hulton Archive/Getty Images, p. 13
(right); © Hulton Archive/Getty Images, pp. 14 (top), 17 (top); The Art Archive/Terry Engell Gallery/Eileen
Tweedy, p. 15; © Jack Novak/SuperStock, p. 18; © Luis Marden/National Geographic/Getty Images,
p. 19 (inset); The Art Archive, p. 22; The Granger Collection, New York, pp. 23 (top), 25 (top), 37, 45;
© Nativestock.com/Marilyn Angel Wynn/Getty Images, p. 26 (inset); © The New York Public Library/Art
Resource, NY, p. 28; The Art Archive/Culver Pictures, p. 31; Library of Congress, pp. 39 (top), 43 (right)
(LC-USZC4-4961); AP Photo/Chitose Suzuki, p. 41 (inset); © SuperStock/SuperStock, p. 44.

Front cover: The Granger Collection, New York. Back cover: © iStockphoto.com/Skip O'Donnell
(background).